CONTENTS

Front cover: An assortment of *Xiphophorus* hybrids. Photo by Dr. Karl Knaack.

Front endpaper: Velvet red swordtails, *Xiphophorus helleri*. Photo courtesy of Wardley Products Co.

Frontis: Hifin *Xiphophorus variatus*. Photo by Dr. Herbert R. Axelrod.

Back endpaper: Sailfin marble molly, *Poecilia latipinna*. Photo by Dr. Herbert R. Axelrod.

Back cover: Blue platies, *Xiphophorus maculatus*. Photo courtesy of Wardley Products Co.

ISBN 0-87666-518-0

Distributed in the U.S. by T.F.H. Publications, Inc., 211 West Sylvania Avenue, PO Box 427, Neptune, NJ 07753; in England by T.F.H. (Gt. Britain) Ltd., 13 Nutley Lane, Reigate, Surrey; in Canada to the book store and library trade by Beaverbooks Ltd., 150 Lesmill Road, Don Mills, Ontario M38 2T5, Canada; in Canada to the pet trade by Rolf C. Hagen Ltd., 3225 Sartelon Street, Montreal 382, Quebec; in Southeast Asia by Y.W. Ong, 9 Lorong 36 Geylang, Singapore 14; in Australia and the South Pacific by Pet Imports Pty. Ltd., P.O. Box 149, Brookvale 2100, N.S.W. Australia; in South Africa by Valid Agencies, P.O. Box 51901, Randburg 2125 South Africa. Published by T.F.H. Publications, Inc., Ltd, the British Crown Colony of Hong Kong.

LIVEBEARERS

BY WILFRED A. WHITERN

Guppies, *Poecilia reticulata,* were one of the first popular fishes in the aquarium hobby and today are more popular than ever. The marbled sailfin molly shown below represents the results of much hybridization and selective breeding. It even carries the lyretail trait. Photo by R. Zukal.

Introduction

The continuing expansion of the tropical fish hobby has created an ever increasing demand by hobbyists for more detailed scientific information. This includes more explicit information on aquarium management, disease control, breeding techniques and nutrition.

Aquarists require this factual information presented at an easy-to-understand level that will alleviate the confusion, frustration and disappointments they so often experience. This book has been specifically written to fulfill that requirement as it applies to the keeping and breeding of

livebearing fishes and is based upon the many advancements in knowledge of that specialized area that have arisen in the past 50 years. These advancements have been the result of the efforts of an increasing number of dedicated hobbyists and scientists who have devoted many tedious hours in an effort to understand the mysteries that constantly confront them.

The species within the livebearer category have always been very popular among hobbyists, especially with beginners, but their tremendous breeding potential has caused an adverse reaction among many aquarists because of the additional equipment and space required. This situation has come about due to indiscriminate mass breeding. As can be expected, there is a general deterioration of fishes bred in this manner, particularly among the livebearing species. Subsequently aquarists tend to lose sight of the primary objective of their hobby—interest and achievement that provides relaxing recreation. This book will help overcome such problems.

Selective breeding has produced a number of different swordtail varieties. (1) The wagtail swordtail has black fins. (2) The tuxedo hifin swordtail carries a broad black body band and the hifin trait first developed in the Simpson swordtail. (3) Extreme fin elongation has rendered the gonopodium of some swordtails useless. Photos by R. Zukal.

3

A giant sailfin molly, *Poecilia velifera*, threatens the male behind it by spreading its huge dorsal sail. The swordtails shown below are very close in coloration to the original wild green swordtails from which most domesticated strains arose. Photo courtesy of Wardley Products Co.

Classification

Classification is a very complex scientific procedure but, for the purpose of this book, will be approached at a very broad and basic level. Using some of the facets of reproduction as the basis of classification, for our purposes we can divide fishes into two distinct groups: those that expel their eggs from the body prior to fertilization and incubation (these are referred to as egglayers) and those whose eggs are fertilized and hatch within the body (these are referred to as livebearers). The former are known as *oviparous* fishes and the latter are known as *ovoviviparous* fishes.

While there are a number of livebearing fishes occurring in freshwater and saltwater habitats in many parts of the world, as aquarium hobbyists we are primarily concerned with four families of livebearers, three of which occur in warm fresh and brackish waters of North, Central and South America. Of the American livebearers, the majority are members of the family Poeciliidae. It is the members of this family, and two genera in particular, *Poecilia* and *Xiphophorus*, that are of the greatest interest to most tropical fish hobbyists. Included are the fishes known in the hobby as the "big four" livebearers; they are guppies, mollies, platies and swordtails. There are other livebearing fishes that have gained some popularity in the hobby, and many of them belong to other families such as Goodeidae, Hemiramphidae (an Asian group) and Anablepidae. But none of these livebearers have ever enjoyed the popularity of the "big four." For comparative purposes some of the less popular livebearers will be briefly mentioned in this book, but by and large the discussions will be limited to those livebearers that are popular and readily available to hobbyists.

3

(1) A male *Poecilia (Limia) nigrofasciata* (commonly known as the humpback limia) courts a female. (2) With his gonopodium aimed forward, the male limia approaches the female from behind and below. (3) A female hump-back limia gives birth to young that are ready to swim as soon as they are born. Photos by Warthoe.

A *Nomorhamphus celebensis* being born head first. The male *N. celebensis* (upper fish in photo below) is easily distinguished from the female by its brighter color pattern and more prominent lower jaw appendage. Photos by H.J. Richter.

Reproduction

Undoubtedly, the thrill of having fishes reproduce in captivity causes aquarists, particularly beginners, to become ardent livebearer enthusiasts. The popularity of livebearers lies in the fact that propagation is effected without any special effort on the part of the aquarist and without special aquarium set-ups . . . the fishes just do what comes naturally. Most aquarium livebearers are prolific breeders.

SEX DIFFERENCES

One reason for the great popularity of livebearers, especially among beginners, is undoubtedly the ease with which they can be sexed. This makes it quite easy for an inexperienced hobbyist to select a breeding pair without having to buy a dozen fish and hope for the best, as is necessary with so many hobby fishes. Male poeciliids have several anal fin rays modified in shape and used to transfer packets of sperm to females. This modified fin is called a *gonopodium*. It is positioned when not in use so that it points toward the rear of the fish. However, when courting and subsequent mating occurs, the gonopodium of most poeciliids can be swung in any direction necessary to effect fertilization—this includes even swinging it forward.

There have been several schools of thought as to whether or not the gonopodium is actually inserted into the female's vent. However, recent advancements in scanning electron microphotography techniques have revealed some interesting facts about the structure of the gonopodium, and these facts may soon clear up all the mystery about fertilization in livebearers. At one time it was believed that the gonopodium was a hollow tube that delivered sperm into the female, or at least toward her genital opening. Scanning electron microphotographs, however, have revealed that in most of the livebearers with which we in the hobby are concerned the gonopodium is grooved along its upper surface, and there is a hook-like structure at the tip of the organ. The terminal "hook" is thought to serve as a means of enabling the male to hold onto the female's genital pore, and it has been proposed that the grooved tube then serves as a "launching ramp" from which the sperm are directed toward the female's opening. Based upon the structure revealed by the microphotographs this seems to be a very plausible explanation of how fertilization comes about in these fishes.

The length of the gonopodium and the specific arrangement of grooves, notches, serrations and the terminal hook vary from one species to another. In some of the domesticated, long-finned strains of livebearers the gonopodium is so long that the males are often incapable of fertilization. In these strains fertilization is possible only by artificial insemination and can usually be done only by professional breeders.

In fishes belonging to the families Goodeidae and Hemiramphidae only the first few rays of the anal fin form the so-called gonopodium. The anal fin therefore appears notched with the forward part somehow carrying out the sexual function. This fin modification obviously lacks the mobility of the gonopodium of poeciliids. *Anableps* has the entire anal fin forming a cylindrical intromittent organ.

The female, of course, lacks the gonopodium and has a "normal" anal fin. Slightly above and forward of the vent the female has a dark area that is called the *gravid spot*. The gravid spot enlarges and darkens in color as embryos develop within the fish's body. This spot can be easily observed except in those fishes whose dark body color conceals it. In black mollies, for instance, the gravid spot cannot be seen. But in addition to lacking the gonopodium, the body of a female livebearer is usually much stouter than that of a male.

In most swordtail strains there is one additional clue as to which fish is which sex. It is usually the male that bears the "sword" at the bottom of the caudal fin. Guppies offer another clue . . . it is usually the male that has all or most of the brilliant colors and fancy fins, although some very ornate females are being produced these days.

MATING
Male livebearers are usually somewhat aggressive toward their own kind. In addition to constant sham battles with other males (these battles rarely result in any serious

(1) Male sailfin mollies, *Poecilia velifera.* (2) A pair of pike livebearers, *Belonesox belizanus.* Photo by H.J. Richter. (3) A closeup of the gonopodium of a male pike livebearer. Photo by H.J. Richter.

damage), males almost continuously chase females. Not only do males court females of their own kind, but they often court (and rather aggressively) females of other livebearer species as well. The latter sometimes leads to successful hybridization, which is why swordtails and platies or different strains of the same species should not be mixed in the same tank if pure strains of offspring are desired.

Mating among livebearers is usually strictly random and polygamous. There is no pairing off as there is, for instance, in substrate-brooding cichlids. The male courts the female by spreading his fins about as far as they can go without splitting the thin tissue between the fin rays. His colors become greatly intensified, and he vigorously swims back and forth in front of and alongside the female. At times he may stop his swimming motion, and with his fins spread he twists his body into an "S" shape while his whole body quivers. As he approaches the female from the side and below, the gonopodium is turned toward the vent of the female. If the female is submissive, contact is made and lasts for two to five or six seconds, depending upon the species and, of course, individual differences. If the female is not submissive, she usually swims away and the male's gonopodium returns to its normal position. The male may then pursue another female or the same female as he starts the courting activities all over again.

The eggs are fertilized within the body of the female, and there all embryonic development takes place. Each embryo receives its nutrition from its own egg yolk. In most poeciliids there is no embryonic nutrition supplied by the mother. However, in at least one family of livebearers, specificially the Goodeidae, the mother does provide the developing embryos with energy during the latter part of the gestation period.

The gestation period of poeciliids lasts from four to eight weeks. Variances in the duration of this period and in the number of eggs developed occur between different species and even between individuals of each species. Individual differences are based upon prevailing environmental conditions such as food, temperature, water chemistry and the age and size of the female. The specifics for each species regarding the duration of the gestation period and the number of fry will be covered later on.

With poeciliids and some of the other livebearers the packets of sperm injected by the male can be stored in the body of the female for quite some time. This means that there can be a few subsequent fertilizations long after there has been any contact between a male and a female. A female can give birth to four or five broods following the proper gestation period for each brood without ever being anywhere near a male, once the initial contact is made. In some of the other families of livebearers there must be contact between a male and a female for each batch of eggs that is to be fertilized, because females of these families do not store sperm. Goodeids and hemiramphids are typical of the latter.

LIVE BIRTH

The moving of a pregnant female that is very close to the time she is due to give birth has been associated with premature hatching of the eggs within the female and, subsequently, premature birth. In this situation the fry are usually born dead, and the chances for the survival of those few premature young that are born alive are not very good. Assuming that all other environmental conditions are correct, losses of young due to premature birth can usually be avoided by not moving the female if she is too close to the due date. Later on in this book you'll find out what gestation period to expect for each species. With that information it is possible to know when the female should not be moved to another tank: she should not be moved when she is closer than 10 days to her probable due date.

1

2

3

(1, 2, and 3) The birth of a guppy. (1) The baby emerges from the birth canal in a curled up position. (2) It quickly uncurls and begins to swim away. (3) The newborn baby guppy heads for the surface where it fills the swim bladder with air. Photos by R. Zukal. (4) A newborn halfbeak baby is quite large compared to the guppy baby. Photo by H.J. Richter. (5) A newborn baby swordtail and mother.

The fry must be protected from cannibalism by the mother when they are born. There are two ways to do this. If the female is of a small species such as a guppy or a platy, she can be placed in a plastic trap that is usually mounted over the edge within a larger tank. These traps are not very roomy. They usually measure about eight inches long, four inches wide and four inches deep. A larger fish such as a swordtail or a molly would not survive the next 10 days very well in such a confined space. The bottom of the trap is made of either closely spaced bars that allow the fry to drop out but keep the female in, or of two flat pieces forming a V-shaped bottom with a slot down the center at the base of the V. The latter more or less guides the newborn young down through the slot and into the outer aquarium. This type of trap seems to do a better job of preventing the fry from swimming back into the trap than the one with the barred bottom. On the other hand, the trap with the barred bottom allows the young to escape faster before they are consumed by the mother. Which trap you choose is a matter of individual preference.

Another way of protecting the young from their cannibalistic mother is to place the female into an aquarium that is heavily planted with a lot of bushy, fine-leaved vegetation, especially the kinds that float at the top, because the surface is usually the first place the fry go to when they are born. The vegetation provides an abundance of hiding places for the newborn fry. Suitable plants for this purpose are *Egeria densa* (which is also known as elodea, ditch moss or anacharis), *Ceratophyllum* or hornwort, *Cabomba* and *Myriophyllum* or water milfoil. Some of these plants should be allowed to float free, and some should be planted so that the fry will have protection at all levels in the tank. Using this method, the female can then be moved to another tank once she has finished giving birth.

In most species, the fry are usually born head first. Sometimes they emerge from the mother's vent in a straight position, but sometimes they come out curled up. With a quick twitch, the latter immediately straighten out. Usually right after they are ejected from the mother's vent the fry head for the surface. Once they reach the top, the swim bladder is filled with air through the pneumatic duct. After initial contact with the atmosphere is made and the swim bladder filled, the fishes are then independent of the atmosphere as far as filling and emptying the swim bladder is concerned. From that time on it is done via the circulatory system. The newborn livebearer can now regulate its buoyancy the same way an adult does.

The size of newborn livebearers varies with each species. Guppies are among the smallest poeciliid fry; the largest are mollies, some of which can exceed three-eighths of an inch at birth. But even guppies are large enough to hunt down newly hatched brine shrimp as their first food.

Egeria densa, commonly called anacharis, is one of the best plants for the livebearer tank as its dense fine-leaved stems provide good protective cover for the newborn young. Photo by Dr. D. Sculthorpe.

Albino swordtails are one of the most delicate swordtail strains. The photo below shows a pair of marigold swordtails. These beautiful fish are highly sought after by livebearer enthusiasts. Photo by Dr. Herbert R. Axelrod.

The Aquarium Environment

In recent years there have been great advances in aquarium technology, including chemical testing equipment that is inexpensive and easy to use and filtering systems whose efficiency is nothing short of amazing. Thus, by good filtration and proper chemical regulation it is now possible for the average aquarist to maintain an artificial environment for his fishes that is immaculately clean, almost to the point of being sterile, and disease-free. The accessibility of this equipment and the ease of its use have no doubt greatly benefited the aquarium hobby in terms of the sturdiness and magnificent coloration of some

of the new strains of domestically raised aquarium fishes. The availability of this new equipment and all of the subsequent progress made as a result of its use have also, however, promoted a lot of misunderstanding regarding the environmental requirements of aquarium fishes. This may be due in part to an overemphasis on the importance of having a nearly sterile aquarium environment. Not given enough emphasis is the great adaptability that most aquarium fishes have to a variety of environmental conditions. A look at the environmental requirements of livebearers will help the hobbyist understand how to handle today's highly sophisticated domestic strains.

THE AQUARIUM

Because some aquarium livebearers, especially the domesticated strains, may be a little bit more sensitive to environmental pollution than most other common aquarium fishes, it is essential that livebearers not be crowded. Some of them, the ones coming from highly oxygenated upland streams have fairly high oxygen requirements. Furthermore, they are, by and large, heavy-bodied fishes, which means that they consume more oxygen and produce more waste than fishes of comparable length but thinner girth such as tetras or killifishes. Most livebearers lead fairly active lives, which means that they probably consume more oxygen and produce more carbon dioxide than relatively sedentary fishes of the same size such as some catfishes. All of this points to the fact that livebearers need a lot of room in the aquarium. To provide a formula for the number of inches of fish per gallon would be pure folly, because the formulated number can be changed by many variables, such as pH, hardness, oxygenation, filtration, feeding, age of the fishes, water temperature and many more.

As a broad generalization, one fish per gallon of water

would normally ensure that each fish has plenty of oxygen and that almost any filtration system is adequate if good aquarium management practices are followed in every other respect. This estimate, however, can vary considerably, depending upon what species is being kept and how old they are as well as how long the hobbyist intends to keep them in that aquarium. For instance, a 10-gallon aquarium might be more than adequate for 25 to 50 juvenile guppies or 25 young platies for a while, but as they grow their numbers should be reduced if they are to achieve their full growth potential. Eight to ten full grown platies or four to six full grown swordtails would be a conservative and sensible limit for a 10-gallon aquarium.

It is also important to remember that any livebearer aquarium should be kept tightly covered. Many a fine livebearer has been lost when the fishes found their way out of an aquarium through a ¼-inch opening between the cover and are especially prone to jumping if the aquarium environment has in some way gone awry.

The amount and kind of light over the aquarium are not important as long as it is not excessively bright and is turned off for at least five or six hours a day. Livebearers generally are not shy fishes, so bright light will not spook them. The only caution to be exercised here is that the aquarium should not become overheated by a strong incandescent light fixture or by an excess of natural sunlight. The best lighting can be provided by locating the aquarium so that it receives at least five or six hours of direct sunlight each day from an east-facing window and supplementing this with artificial illumination from an overhead fluorescent light fixture, using one of the special plant-growing bulbs such as Penn-Plax's Aquari-lux.® Intensity and duration of the illumination should be based on the requirements of the plants being grown in the tank and not on the requirements of the fishes.

An assortment of platies *(Xiphophorus maculatus).* (1) Red platies are an old favorite among aquarium hobbyists. (2) This is a wagtail brushtail platy which is always an attraction at tropical fish shows. Photo by S. Kochetov. (3) The red wagtail platy is a favorite livebearer among beginners. Photo by K. Quitschau. (4) These platies show the comet pattern in the tail. Photo by M.F. Roberts.

The aquarium should be located in a place where it will not be subject to chills or drafts. This is especially important with livebearers because, although they can take more exposure to cooler water than many aquarium fishes can, they are extremely sensitive to a sudden temperature change, particularly where the change is a downward drop.

THE WATER

Water chemistry is one subject in the maintenance of livebearers about which much conflict has arisen. The proponents of one school of thought claim that the water for livebearers should be acidic and even amber tinted by an abundance of organic acids such as those derived from peat moss. Proponents of another school of thought claim that livebearers can only be kept successfully in hard alkaline water. Neither case is in fact altogether true. Even though domesticated fancy livebearers are in many cases very far removed from their wild progenitors in physical appearance, they still have the same habitat requirements. Let's take a brief look at the natural habitats of the ancestors of our highly domesticated livebearers to help us gain some understanding of our aquarium fishes' requirements.

Fishes of the genus *Poecilia* which includes guppies (*Poecilia reticulata*) and mollies (*Poecilia latipinna, P. velifera, P. sphenops* and others) are generally found in freshwater and brackish water streams, rivers, ponds, lakes, swamps and even drainage ditches located in coastal areas. These waters usually contain more salt and minerals than that found in inland freshwater habitats, thus they are fairly hard and alkaline. Sometimes these waters, and especially the stagnant waters of the swamps and canals, have an amber tint. This is because they contain a high amount of dissolved organic materials due to the excessive decomposition of leaf litter in tropical and subtropical climates. One tends to associate amber-colored water that is high in organics with the soft acidic conditions found in some tropical rivers such as the Rio Negro in Brazil, but this is not so in the coastal waters of the tropics. Many of these coastal streams and lakes flow over beds of limestone, and many of them are often inundated by seawater, thus even with the amber color these waters are still hard and alkaline, albeit they may not be as alkaline as the coastal waters that are low in dissolved organics.

Because of the water conditions in their natural habitats, poeciliids, especially mollies, should be kept in hard alkaline water that is slightly salty or brackish. This slight degree of salinity can be introduced into their aquarium water by dissolving one to two tablespoons of non-iodized table salt, aquarium salt or sea salt mix into each gallon of water. The sea salt mix gives the best results because it includes many of the important trace minerals that are found in the natural waters of these fishes.

As far as pH is concerned, any water that is neutral (7.0) to slightly alkaline suits these fishes well. A pH of 7.5 to 7.8 is not too severe for guppies and mollies—especially mollies. The dissolving of salt in the water tends to keep the pH at neutral or a bit higher as long as uneaten food and other organic debris is removed from the water as soon as it is detected. A temporary or carbonate hardness of 12 to 20 DH suits them fine. The salt also tends to maintain a high temporary hardness level. In other words, guppies and mollies do well in ordinary tapwater drawn from most urban supplies, with a little bit of salt added.

Fishes of the genus *Xiphophorus* (the swordtails and platies) are generally found not in coastal waters having a high salt content, but in lowland backwaters such as swamps and lakes as well as in highland springs, lakes and rivers. They are also often found in cool lagoons. These waters are not characteristically high in organics although the more stagnant waters are. Most of these waters are, however, characteristically high in dissolved minerals. This means that swordtails *(Xiphophorus helleri)*, platies *(X. maculatus)* and variatus *(X. variatus)* also generally come from waters that are fairly hard and slightly alkaline.

There are, of course, exceptions with most of the live-bearers. There are, no doubt, some variants of these fishes that are found in acidic waters, but they are few and far between. These exceptions, however, attest to the wide environmental tolerance of these fishes where water chemistry is concerned, thus making them easy to keep in captivity as long as their temperature, space and food requirements are met. That is why some hobbyists have had great success with guppies, for instance, by keeping them in amber-colored acidic water.

As unimportant as precise water chemistry is to success in keeping most livebearers, the opposite is true where the control of water temperatures is concerned. Aquarium livebearers *must* have unfluctuating temperatures if they are to survive without having constant bouts with diseases such as ich, velvet and others.

Mollies and guppies generally require temperatures in the high 70's to low 80's. Hobbyists have found, however, that where sailfin mollies are concerned, the males do not develop high dorsal sails if they are raised in water that is at the high end of their range of tolerance. Therefore, sailfin mollies should be kept as cool as possible within their range of tolerance when they are young. A temperature of 75 to 76°F. is just about ideal for most sailfin mollies.

Xiphophorus species generally do best at temperatures ranging from 72 to 79°F. Swordtails prefer the mid to high end of this range, but most platies prefer and do better at the low end.

In a community tank containing fishes of various types, it is usually the livebearers that are the first ones to succumb to diseases that can be brought on by chilling. Therefore, what is most important as far as the temperature requirements of livebearers is concerned is that the fishes not be subjected to sudden drops in temperature of even a few degrees. To avoid this possibility, make sure that the aquarium heater you have selected is sized adequately for your aquarium and is a good quality piece of equipment (very cheap heaters usually are erratic in their control).

FILTRATION AND AERATION

Because of the relatively high oxygen requirements of livebearers, fairly strong filtration and aeration are required in their aquaria, and by setting the equipment up properly both filtration and aeration can be taken care of by the same piece of equipment. Undergravel filtration is recommended for both its filtering efficiency and ability to oxygenate the water quite adequately. In order for it to do so, however, it must be set up properly.

The newer undergravel filters having wide diameter riser tubes are the most efficient. They employ an airstone at the bottom of each riser tube that sends a stream of medium-size bubbles up the tubes and moves a maximum amount of water through the system. The riser tubes must be extended all the way to the surface of the water and an elbow installed at the top of the tube. This directs the filtered water across the surface which produces strong surface turbulence and maximum water circulation in the tank. Good surface turbulence is most important in providing livebearers with all the oxygen they need, for it is at the surface that most oxygen is dissolved into the water. Here, too, is where carbon dioxide and other waste gases are released from the water. Without the surface turbulence, very little of the carbon dioxide escapes from the water, and livebearers are very sensitive to the effects of a high concentration of carbon dioxide in the water. It is also most important that no less than two inches of gravel of a medium particle size be placed over the undergravel filter plate. This provides an adequate substrate for the proliferation of the beneficial bacteria that break down the copious amounts of ammonia produced by livebearers as a waste product.

Outside power filters can also be used either alone or as a supplement to the undergravel filter. These are very efficient mechanical filters and if set up properly can also be very good oxygenators. The filter should be set up with the return stream flowing across the surface of the water for the same reasons that the undergravel filter is set up that way.

PLANTS AND AQUARIUM DECOR

It is not necessary to provide livebearers with rock caves, for they are not shy fishes and they are not territorial. They are active swimmers and browsers and will not usually utilize such decor for its concealment value. However, they do need to have an abundance of plants in the tank for several reasons. Being browsers or grazers, livebearers are constantly picking over the surfaces in the aquarium looking for algae and for microorganisms living among the algal strands. The growth of live plants in the aquarium promotes the chemical and physical conditions necessary for the growth of these organisms. Furthermore, the plants themselves are an essential part of the diet of these fishes. For this reason, fine-leaved plants should be used so that the fishes can forage on them without totally destroying them. One further use for plants in the livebearer aquarium is to provide shelter for the young so they can hide from their cannibalistic parents, although this generally is not too much of a problem if the parent fish are kept well fed.

Ideal plants for the livebearer aquarium are cabomba *(Cabomba caroliniana)*, hygrophila *(Hygrophila polysperma)*, *Myriophyllum*, hornwort *(Ceratophyllum)*, watersprite *(Ceratopteris thalicroides)*, anacharis or elodea *(Egeria densa)* and liverwort *(Riccia fluitans)*.

Liverwort is most often seen as a floating plant. It forms a dense thicket at the surface and provides excellent shelter for newborn livebearers. It is a favorite of those livebearers that like to nibble on vegetation. The plant is not very exacting in its water chemistry and light requirements but will fall apart and decompose in tanks that are overly rich in nutrients. In the aquarium, *Riccia fluitans* goes into a dormant state during the winter. In order to keep the plant flourishing, it should be allowed to hibernate during the winter. This can be done by placing some of it in a special tank or even a one-gallon jar and allowing it to receive only natural sunlight and not supplementing it with artificial illumination. You can continue to use the liverwort in the breeding tank with normal illumination, and by the time it deteriorates due to the lack of a dormant period there will be a fresh batch to start the regrowth with.

Another plant that does exceptionally well in the aquarium as a floating plant is hornwort *(Ceratophyllum demersum)*. Its multiple whorls of fine leaves and its highly-branched structure provide good shelter for livebearer fry. It is a strong plant that thrives in almost any water. One hornwort species, *Ceratophyllum submersum,* even thrives well in brackish water, making it an almost ideal plant for a molly tank.

There are several *Myriophyllum* or water milfoil species that flourish quite well in a typical livebearer aquarium. However, rather than just left floating in the tank, these plants seem to thrive a bit better, even though they don't root very well, if they are planted in the bottom substrate. Planted in clusters along the back and sides of the aquarium, they grow to the surface, thus providing plenty of cover for the fry yet leaving plenty of swimming room in the tank for the adults. One of the most readily available species is *Myriophyllum spicatum*.

Elodea *(Egeria densa)* or ditch moss or anacharis as it is known in some places is an excellent plant for the livebearer tank. It grows well floating or planted in almost any kind of water, but it does require fairly strong light to flourish. Its fine-leaved stems provide excellent cover, and the leaves are soft enough to provide forage.

Hygrophila polysperma is a readily available plant that is planted in thick bunches and provides good shelter and forage for livebearers. It roots very strongly and grows to the surface when provided with strong illumination. Its many small lanceolate leaves provide plenty of hiding places for fry. It can survive in most aquarium water conditions including brackish water. In addition to having great utility in the livebearer tank, *Hygrophila polysperma* is a highly decorative plant.

Water sprite *(Ceratopteris thalicroides)* can be useful plant in the livebearer aquarium. It is a fern that flourishes in soft, acidic, well-shaded water, but it is quite adaptable to a variety of conditions. It will survive in a tank that contains neutral to slightly alkaline water and that is moderately illuminated, but, of course, it will not flourish in these conditions. The plant grows in several forms. The most useful to the livebearer enthusiast is its floating form. It forms floating thickets with dense bushy roots that hang down into the water. The roots and thick mat of surface leaves provide excellent shelter for newborn livebearer fry. The leaves of this plant are quite soft and make excellent forage for mollies and other plant-loving livebearers.

In using plants of the type discussed so far, it is important to remember that all of them take most of their nutrition from the water and will not thrive very well in an aquarium that has just been set up no matter how perfect all other environmental conditions are. After the aquarium has been in use for about six months these plants can be added to the tank; then and only then will they flourish.

There are, however, other plants that can survive fairly well in a newly set up aquarium. Usually plants having a thick rhizome or rootstock will do well in such a tank, because they carry their own food supply in the rhizome. These plants can subsist on their own food supply until there has been sufficient time to build up a supply of nutrients in the water and in the substrate. Plants such as the Java fern *(Microsorium pteropus)* or some of the sword-plants such as *Echinodorus cordifolius* have heavy rootstocks and will do well in the newly set up tank. The *Echinodorus* species, however, must have strong illumination, but this is generally not a problem, for livebearers flourish in tanks that are well lit as well as in tanks whose illumination is on the dim side. The only problem with these plants is that they do not provide the cover that fine-leaved plants do, so they are not especially useful except for their decorative value.

The livebearer enthusiast would do well to consider using some artificial foliage in the newly set up aquarium. Many of the fine-leaved types are available in realistic-looking plastic imitations. These provide baby livebearers with the protection they need and can be used until such time that the tank has aged enough to support a growth of live fine-leaved plants.

The livebearer aquarium should be decorated with an assortment of bushy plants in order to provide protection for the harassed females and newborn young. Photo by R. Zukal.

A pike livebearer swallows a full-grown guppy. This predatory livebearer is capable of swallowing very large prey, therefore it must be kept in its own aquarium. Photo by R. Zukal. The fish below are another species of sailfin molly, *Poecilia petenensis*. Photo by Sam Dunton, New York Zoological Society.

Foods and Feeding Practices

The key to a fully nutritious diet is variety. No fish thrives well on a continuous diet consisting of only one kind of food. The necessary variety can be achieved by using an assortment of commercially prepared dry foods supplemented with assorted live, frozen and freeze-dried foods.

Quantity as well as quality in the diet is an important factor in raising healthy robust fishes. A variety of good foods fed in the wrong quantity and at the wrong time can have drastic effects on the health of aquarium fishes. Remember that the digestive system of tropical fishes is small compared to the size of their body. Therefore, only a small amount of food at a time is necessary to satisfy their needs.

But this food is digested rather quickly, and the fishes are ready to eat again not very long after the last feeding. For this reason, fishes should be fed small quantities of food several times a day rather than a larger quantity once a day.

Because tropical fishes can only eat small amounts of food at a time, they usually stop eating when they are full. If a lot of uneaten food is left in the tank, it will spoil very quickly and thus remain uneaten. This fouls the water and interferes with the biological and chemical balance of the aquarium system. A fouled aquarium system promotes the growth of disease organisms such as certain types of bacteria and fungi and promotes the proliferation of other disease organisms that are detrimental to the health of fishes and plants. An excess of decomposing organic matter also competes with the fishes for oxygen. Not only does it deprive the fishes of oxygen, but it also causes an increase in the amount of carbon dioxide that is dissolved in the water, and this results in drastic changes in the chemistry of the water, often dropping the pH well below the level that most fishes can tolerate. The best way to avoid an excess of decomposing organic matter in an aquarium is to avoid overfeeding the fishes.

A variety of dry foods can and should be used as the basic diet, but these *must* be supplemented with other types of foods. For clarification, foods for fishes can be classified into four groups: dry foods, cultured and collected live foods, frozen foods and freeze-dried foods. Let's look at these groups of foods one at a time to see what each comprises.

Dry foods: These are available in several different forms as well as in numerous varieties. Dry foods can be purchased in pelleted, granulated and flake forms, the flake forms being the most popular. In these forms one finds specific kinds of foods such as shrimp, squid and green vegetable foods. Additionally, there are a number of different kinds of food mixtures that consist of the single food items just mentioned as well as many other ingredients.

These mixtures are blended for specific purposes such as growth promotion, color promotion, conditioning, etc. It is advisable to keep at least four or five different kinds of these foods on hand at all times and use them as the basis of the diet, feeding at least one of them once every day.

Cultured and collected live foods: It's a bit more trouble to keep a supply of living foods handy for your fishes but it's well worth the little bit of extra effort it requires for the reward it produces. The inclusion of live foods in the diet produces much healthier and much more robust fishes than does a diet without live foods.

One of the easiest live foods to culture is brine shrimp. The newly hatched nauplii are just about the right size for newborn livebearer fry. Brine shrimp eggs can be purchased from a pet dealer and easily hatched in a salt solution. This nutritious food can be used in raising livebearers until the fishes are at least three months of age and even up to adulthood in the case of smaller species such as guppies and platies. In the proper culture solution, the brine shrimp nauplii can be raised to a larger size for use as food for the larger subadult and adult livebearers, and even smaller livebearer species can eat adult brine shrimp. Some dealers sell live adult brine shrimp.

Microworms are another useful food for newborn livebearers. These are roundworms or nematode worms that are a bit smaller than newly hatched brine shrimp nauplii. They can be easily cultured in damp baby cereal.

Tubifex worms are often sold in pet shops. They are small thin relatives of the earthworm. They are not easy to culture, but they are inexpensive and nutritious, so a small amount of them can be purchased weekly. Tubifex worms should be well rinsed before feeding them to your fishes, as they do tend to carry bacteria species that could harm your fishes.

White worm cultures are sold in pet shops during the fall and winter. These, too, are small thin relatives of the earthworm, but they are cleaner than tubifex and are easily cultured in a small box of soil.

Vestigial-winged or "wingless" fruitflies are sometimes sold in cultures by live-food dealers. They are also easy to raise and highly nutritious for livebearers who feed on them quite greedily.

There are some live foods that are not usually sold by tropical fish dealers but are easy to collect. One of the most nutritious of these is mosquito larvae. During late spring, summer and early fall they are easily netted from shallow stagnant ponds or pools. Midge larvae commonly known as bloodworms can be collected on the bottom of the same pools in which mosquito larvae are found. In the wintertime glassworms or phantom midge larvae can be collected from under the ice of shallow woodland ponds. Another very popular live food, and one that sometimes finds its way into pet shops, is *Daphnia* or water fleas. They can be seined from ponds that are not heavily populated with fishes, and young *Daphnia* can be sifted out for younger fishes. One of the most easily collected and most nutritious of all live foods is earthworms. To feed them to livebearers, simply chop them into fine pieces using a single-edge razor blade. All of these live foods are highly nutritious and produce spectacular results, making it worth the effort to collect them. Detailed information on collecting and culturing live foods can be found in *Encyclopedia of Live Foods* by Charles O. Masters.

Frozen foods: A wide variety of frozen tropical fish foods are available in tropical fish shops. Frozen foods such as clam, squid, mussel, beef heart, bloodworms, mosquito larvae and young and adult brine shrimp make up the dealer's menu. All of these foods are very nutritious, and it is suggested that three or four different kinds be kept on hand and rotated into the diet on a regular daily basis.

Freeze-dried foods: Tubifex, brine shrimp and plankton are available in this form. These foods are not overly expensive. They are convenient, nutritious and keep indefinitely. It is suggested that at least one kind of freeze-dried food be worked into your fishes' diet on a regular basis.

In this chapter it has been emphasized that success with livebearers can only be achieved if there is a great amount of variety in the diet. This, of course, applies to almost any kind of fish but is especially important for some of the highly domesticated strains of livebearers that are not nearly as sturdy as their wild progenitors. If fishes are fed only one or two kinds of foods, dietary deficiencies are bound to cause one form or another of malnutrition.

While the nutritional requirements of fishes are well known, the specific nutrient composition of many of their food items is not well known. By feeding fishes a wide variety of foods, the chances of their receiving all of their required nutrients are increased. Variety in the diet gives fishes a broad array of proteins, fats, carbohydrates, vitamins and minerals. Without adequate carbohydrates, for instance, many of the proteins consumed by fishes cannot be properly utilized. A deficiency in the vitamin thiamine can cause poor appetite, convulsions, loss of equilibrium, muscle degeneration, skin defects, loss of color and poor growth. Other vitamin deficiencies can cause neurological disorders or disorders of various organ systems. A mineral deficiency can cause bone deformations such as spinal curvature.

Excesses of a particular nutrient can cause almost as many problems as a deficiency. For instance, an excess of carbohydrates causes digestive disorders and obesity, and obesity can cause many of the same problems in fishes that it causes in humans. A regular feeding schedule consisting of an assortment of food types assures that your fishes will not suffer from malnutrition and will keep them healthy enough to make them resistant to many of the disease organisms that "normally" invade the aquarium.

The swordtail on the left is suffering from an extreme case of tail rot. This disease can often be successfully treated by adding antibiotics to the water. The humped back and rough appearance of the swordtail below indicates that it is a victim of old-age.

Diseases: Prevention, Diagnosis, Cure

Lack of proper care and understanding of the fundamentals required for good aquarium management are the basic reasons for the majority of the common disease outbreaks in the livebearer aquarium. It has been mentioned that most aquarium livebearers are a bit more sensitive to environmental stress than are the majority of tropical fish species commonly kept in the aquarium, and mollies are especially sensitive.

It has been mentioned several times that good diet, plenty of space and steady temperature promote good health in livebearers. One other important factor in maintaining these fishes in prime condition is frequent water changing.

Water changing is indeed important with all aquarium fishes, but especially so with livebearers because of their high sensitivity to pollutants. Combined with other good aquarium management practices, a 25% weekly water change should virtually eliminate outbreaks of most of the common aquarium fish diseases such as ich, velvet and fungal and bacterial finrot. Healthy fishes are capable of resisting these diseases, but fishes that are in poor overall condition or are being kept in a stressed or incorrect environment are not very resistant to these diseases. Frequent water changing helps dilute organic pollutants in the water that arise from fish and plant wastes, thus keeping the concentration of these pollutants below a level that can affect the fishes and below the level that encourages the proliferation of disease organisms.

Many fine fish specimens can be cured of a disease if all the necessary equipment and medications are immediately available. Delay may cause the disease to spread to such proportions that a normally therapeutic dose of the chosen medication may not be effective. However, it is never advisable to try to hurry a cure for any disease; many diseases have a specific time cycle, and the application of additional medication beyond the recommended dosage will not hasten the cure. Furthermore, it can be dangerous to use larger than prescribed doses for any given medicant. Many of them contain ingredients that are harmless to the fish if used as prescribed, but dosages in excess of the prescribed amount can sometimes be lethal. The same idea usually applies to the use of two or more medicants at one time. Their effects can sometimes nullify each other or they can act synergistically, often to the detriment of the fish. In other words, the drugs can have effects when used together that they don't have when used separately, and these effects can be lethal to the fishes.

Never gamble with a disease, especially if you've just spent a year or two developing a new strain of livebearer or improving an old strain. If the disease strikes in an aquarium and is contagious, remove all the fish immediately and place them in isolation, separating those that already have visible signs of the disease into one tank and those that are still free of the symptoms into another tank. The aquarium from which the diseased fishes were removed should be stripped down. The sand or gravel should be sterilized in a strong saline solution by adding as much non-iodized salt as will dissolve in the aquarium water and allowing it to remain in the tank for about 24 hours. The tank can then be thoroughly rinsed. Commercial sterilizing solutions such as methylene blue are available in pet shops. Plastic plants, heaters, thermometers and virtually all non-organic materials can be left in the tank for sterilization, but be advised that some commercial disinfectants permanently discolor gravel, rocks, plastic plants and other equipment. As another alternative, the gravel can be removed and boiled in water, but the tank and the rest of its contents must still be sterilized. *Do not use hot water in an aquarium,* as it will crack the glass. Live plants can be sterilized by soaking them no longer than five minutes in a solution of alum, a product available from most pharmacies. Mix a teaspoon of alum to each quart of room-temperature water used. The plants should be rinsed thoroughly after a five-minute soak.

It should be remembered that many disease organisms are present even in healthy aquaria and that these organisms will only proliferate when conditions are right for them. A weak or stressed fish is an open invitation to an outbreak of disease. When a fish is under stress of any kind, its reaction is to lose some of its body slime. Under normal conditions a fish's body slime protects it from infection by many different disease organisms, but when the coating of slime becomes thinner than normal or is cast off altogether, the fish is very susceptible to these diseases. Environmental stress is therefore one of the primary causes of disease.

CHEMICAL POISONING

General symptoms of environmental upset should be recognized by the aquarist in order to head off diseases before they break out. If a fish hangs at the surface gasping for air, this is a sure sign that the water has become depleted of oxygen. This is usually due to an excess of organic decomposition in the aquarium. Uneaten foods and dead fish, snails and plants can trigger this condition. The process of organic decomposition consumes oxygen in the water and increases the amount of dissolved carbon dioxide present in the water. Thus the fishes are being asphyxiated. This situation should be rectified immediately by making a partial water change, removing the source of pollution and by temporarily increasing the strength of aeration in the water. The latter causes more oxygen to be dissolved into the water and causes more carbon dioxide to leave the water.

Ammonia poisoning is another result of excess decomposition. Fishes may rub themselves on objects in the aquarium, shake their heads rather violently and breathe in an erratic manner, possibly very rapidly and heavily. Oxygen depletion and carbon dioxide poisoning complicate the situation, because under those conditions fishes are much more sensitive to even minute amounts of ammonia in the water. The cure is the same as it is for carbon dioxide poisoning and oxygen insufficiency. However, if the amount of ammonia is so great that a water change and heavy aeration don't help, then it may be necessary to temporarily lower the pH of the water just a bit. A few drops of household vinegar or an appropriate amount of sodium biphosphate will do the job. Lowering the pH renders the ammonia harmless. The lowering should be done gradually, however, because a sudden drop in pH can be as stressful to a fish as a sudden drop of temperature. Furthermore, if there is an excess of carbon dioxide present, lowering the pH will make that situation worse. A temporary gradual drop in pH to about 6.6 will not permanently harm most livebearers as long as the source of the pollution is removed and the pH is then gradually brought back up to neutral or slightly alkaline after a few days.

Another complication caused by excess organic decomposition in the aquarium is acidosis. This results from a prolonged exposure to extremely acidic conditions which are usually caused by heavy organic decomposition. If fishes are suffering from acidosis they may show hemorrhagic marks on the skin, especially at the fin bases and around the eyes, nostrils and lips. They show rapid and heavy breathing. The fishes lie about the bottom of the tank and may suddenly, on the slightest provocation, begin to madly dash about the aquarium, colliding with everything in sight including each other. Then they come to rest once again on the bottom of the tank or in the crotch of a plant, with almost no signs of breathing at all.

The symptoms of acidosis call for immediate and drastic action. Almost a complete water change is necessary. The pH must be returned to normal *rather quickly*. A gradual elevation of the pH in this case is no more correct than is a gradual adjustment to fresh air for a person who has just had a prolonged exposure to a poisonous gas such as carbon monoxide. Immediate and total withdrawal from feeding is necessary. Normal aeration should be employed, and finally the tank should be completely darkened for a few days by covering the sides and top with black paper. After a few days the paper can be gradually withdrawn and feeding gradually restored, but all will be to no avail if the source of the pollution is not found and eliminated.

Similar symptoms show in fishes that have had a prolonged exposure to water that is too alkaline, and in addition, the fishes may show a grayish white turbidity of the skin. The cure is the same as it is for acidosis, and the source of the excess alkalinity must be found and eliminated. A likely source is a rock or other decorative item.

DROPSY

Dropsy itself is not a disease. Rather, it is a sign of various diseases in which the abdominal cavity fills with fluid. Internal bacterial infection is usually the cause of the condition. A dropsical fish has a swollen abdomen and its scales are raised at an angle to the body. Until recently, more often than not dropsy was not a curable condition. It was realized that dropsy was an internal infection and that medicants should be given to the fish internally, but methods of introducing medicants into fishes were not commonly known until recently. Hobbyists, therefore, depended upon standard medications being absorbed through the skin of the fish. This, of course, does not happen with most commercially available aquarium remedies. There are now, however, several products on the market that can be absorbed into an ailing fish's internal systems through both the skin and the gills. Among them, the furan derivatives are especially effective in treating internal bacterial infections. Standard aquarium antibiotics can be used to treat dropsy if they are put into the fish's food so that they are taken internally. For this method of treatment to be effective, it requires that the aquarist recognize the signs of internal bacterial infection in its very early stages so the fish can be medicated before it loses its appetite. It is suggested that the medicated food be given to other fishes in the tank that are not yet showing signs of the disease. This should effectively prevent the spread of an infectious internal bacterial disease in the aquarium.

There are other kinds of dropsical conditions that are not contagious, and there are still many causes of dropsy that are not curable. If the properly treated fish does not respond positively within a few days, it should be destroyed and properly disposed of.

A constipated or egg-bound female livebearer is often mistakenly treated for dropsy. In either case the abdomen can become severely swollen, but the scales usually do not stand off the body. Both of the latter conditions can usually be rectified by dietary modification. It may be necessary to help a bound up female pass dead eggs and accumulated fecal matter by holding her in a wet net and gently massaging the body from the front toward the rear and down toward the vent.

POPEYE

Exophthalmos or popeye is one of the symptoms of diseases such as *Ichthyophonus* (also called *Ichthyosporidium),* which is an internal fungal disease, bacterial kidney disease and piscine tuberculosis. In popeye, pockets of fluid and sometimes gas build up behind the eyes, thus causing the eyes to bulge outward.

Bacterial kidney disease and piscine tuberculosis can be treated by including wide spectrum antibiotics in the infected fish's food, but the treatment only occasionally cures the disease. Non-infected fishes from the same tank should be treated in the same way to prevent the infection from spreading.

If popeye is caused by *Ichthyophonus,* small white areas will develop on the skin of the infected fish at a later stage of the disease. The disease is not curable, but it is preventable by maintaining immaculately clean aquarium conditions. Infected fishes should be destroyed and properly disposed of.

WHITE SPOT DISEASE (ICH)

There are few if any aquarists who have not had one or more bouts with this highly contagious fish disease. Ich or white spot disease is caused by a protozoan parasite called *Ichthyophthirius multifiliis.* Ich parasites are present in nearly every aquarium, and they remain dormant if the fishes in the tank remain unstressed and in good health. However, when stress occurs, especially the stress caused by a sudden drop in temperature of more than just a few degrees, tropical fishes, and especially livebearers, become highly susceptible to attacks by this fast-spreading disease.

One of the earliest signs of the disease is fishes rubbing themselves on objects in the aquarium. Mollies may tend to exhibit the shimmies as an even earlier symptom. They do so by undulating the body back and forth in an exaggerated swimming motion, but they do not actually move forward. Shimmies seem to be triggered by a chill and may be an early sign of other diseases, too. After a few days, white spots about the size of grains of salt or sugar begin to appear all over the infected fish. The white spots are individual parasites that have imbedded themselves in the victim's skin, fed on the host's body fluids for a few days and have become encysted. After a day or two the cysts start to drop off the host, but of course others are at the same time just beginning to form. The cysts drop to the bottom of the tank and the protozoan within the cyst begins to multiply by division. Finally, after a day or two, the cyst breaks open, releasing as many as 500 new free-swimming ciliated parasites, each immediately seeking a host fish. Familiarity with the life cycle of this parasite makes it easy to understand why this disease spreads so rapidly among aquarium fishes, especially among highly susceptible species such as livebearers. This knowledge also helps one understand how to treat the disease.

The only stage in the life cycle of *Ichthyophthirius multifiliis* in which the parasite is vulnerable to standard treatments is the free-swimming stage. This stage rarely lasts more than 24 hours, but treatment must be continued for no less than 10 days in order to catch all of the parasites in this stage.

There are ways to cure this disease without using chemicals. It has been established that the free-swimming ich parasites cannot survive very long in water that is heated to 86°F. This temperature will not harm the fishes for the necessary 10 days if heavy aeration is maintained. The extra aeration is necessary because at warmer temperatures water holds less dissolved oxygen than it does at cooler temperatures. If the disease is caught in its early stages heat treatment should stop it. A tablespoon of non-iodized salt added to each gallon of water seems to have some effect in stopping the disease when the heat treatment is used. Rather than killing the parasites themselves, the addition of salt may help the fishes to be more resistant to further attack.

In eradicating the disease from the aquarium, extra assurance that the parasites are either gone or returned to a dormant stage can be had by removing all fishes from the aquarium for two to three weeks. Without the availability of hosts the free-swimming parasites will die of starvation. The remaining unattached cysts go into a dormant state and remain there as long as the fishes remain healthy.

For more severe cases of ich, the disease can be treated with a chemical called malachite green. This chemical is available under a number of different trade names and is often mixed in commercial preparations with a wide assortment of other helpful chemicals.

VELVET

Velvet disease is caused by another protozoan parasite called *Oodinium*. The cysts show up on the body of the fish as a velvety golden coating. They are much smaller than the cysts of ich, and accordingly they are much more difficult to detect. The initial symptoms are about the same as those of ich but are not usually as severe. The life cycle of the parasite is about the same as that of ich, but the treatment is a bit different. *Oodinium* parasites do not respond to heat treatment as readily as ich parasites do, and the chemical of choice is acriflavine rather than malachite green. The treatment should be continued for 10 to 15 days so as to kill all free-swimming parasites. Generally, livebearers are not as susceptible to velvet as they are to ich. Furthermore, the disease does not affect the fishes as severely as ich does. Some fishes can survive for quite a long time while carrying velvet parasites. Nonetheless, the disease is highly contagious and eventually is just as debilitating as ich is, so it should be treated as soon as it is recognized.

FIN ROT

Fin rot is probably the second most frequent disease observed by aquarists and is one that can cause great losses if not given immediate attention. The disease usually commences in the caudal fin and rapidly spreads to other fins. The first visual sign of the disease is that the caudal fin becomes ragged along the posterior edge, especially at the tips of the lobes. Shortly after the fins take on the ragged appearance a white edging appears along the ragged margins. Initially fin rot is usually caused by an external bacterial infection, and it can be effectively treated by dissolving a wide spectrum antibiotic such as Tetracycline® in the water. The treatment should, of course, be carried out in an isolation tank since wide spectrum antibiotics also kill the beneficial bacteria in the biofilter.

A secondary development with fin rot is the attack of dead fin tissue by fungi such as *Saprolegnia*. If the disease is not stopped quickly, the fungus spreads to other areas of the body including the mouth. This type of fungus is highly contagious. Other types of fungi also attack the body and the mouth. Fungal hyphae can be noticed on the diseased fish as a cottony growth. In addition to continuing the antibiotic treatment, fishes infected with fungus should be removed from the water and held in a wet net while the infected area is swabbed with Mercurochrome®.

WORMS AND OTHER PARASITES

There are several kinds of worms that attack aquarium fishes, but one of particular concern to livebearer enthusiasts is the intestinal roundworm or nematode called *Camallanus. Camallanus* does attack other fishes, but it is most frequently reported in livebearers. It is a red- or orange-colored worm that lives in the intestine of its host and feeds from its host's blood and other body fluids. The worm is first noticed protruding from the anus of its host.

Camallanus is transmitted to aquarium fishes by *Cyclops* which are, unfortunately, one of the favorite foods of livebearers and are eaten by them in large quantities in the wild. *Cyclops* sometimes find their way into farm ponds which is how domesticated strains of livebearers become infected.

The most effective treatment for a *Camallanus* infestation is a chemical whose generic name is trichlorfon. It is an insecticide used by cattle farmers and wildlife managers. It is sold under the trade name of Dylox® as well as under three or four other popular names, and it is usually carried in veterinary supply stores or farm supply stores. Unfortunately, it is not usually sold in quantities sufficiently small for the treatment of a few fishes, so its use is only practical for the large-scale breeder. For the hobbyist with a few tanks of livebearers, there are several commercial products that are useful in treating a variety of intestinal worms including *Camallanus*.

Another parasite frequently encountered by livebearer enthusiasts is the anchor worm, *Lernaea cyprinacea*. It is not actually a worm at all, but is a modified form of a parasitic copepod. It can also be effectively eradicated with trichlorfon.

There are many other diseases that infect livebearers, and it is not possible to discuss them all in this book. It has been the purpose of this chapter to give you an overview of prevention, diagnosis and treatment of some of the more commonly encountered maladies of livebearers. Much more detailed information on fish diseases is available in Dr. G. Schubert's book *Cure and Recognize Aquarium Fish Diseases*.

Most poeciliid males approach a female from behind and below for mating. These fishes have almost complete mobility of the gonopodium so that it can be thrust forward. A male swordtail with a short sword is often indicative of a young specimen that will grow a much longer sword. Photos by R. Zukal.

Breeding Techniques

Because of their tremendous breeding potential, particularly if permitted to breed without restriction, there is a reasonable expectancy that the aquarist may be constantly faced with the need for additional equipment and space. In such a situation the incentive for interest in the hobby is defeated and the derivation of recreation and relaxation becomes a lost cause.

In the native habitats of livebearers the large volumes of water contain abundant supplies of food-size living organisms and beneficial dissolved mineral salts and have fairly constant temperatures. These conditions permit the prolific breeding of these fishes without a high potential for

deterioration of any given species. In captivity, however, the conditions caused by an exceedingly smaller volume of water lacking the full complement of living organisms and dissolved minerals and having highly fluctuating temperatures result in many damaging effects when prolific breeding occurs. In the limited confines of an aquarium it is easy for brothers and sisters to mate frequently, and usually at an immature age. This inevitably and ultimately leads to a great amount of deterioration of the stock involved.

It cannot be overemphasized that this system of uncontrolled breeding undertaken in captivity in a haphazard manner can produce problems of such magnitude as to cause the aquarist to entirely lose interest in the hobby, as his once beautiful domesticated strains revert to their wild ancestral forms. However, if the breeding of livebearers is undertaken by a selective system of controlled procedures, there is a great possibility of improving each stock involved. Such a system also provides incentive toward a specific achievement that automatically enlarges itself, thus causing the aquarist to become more and more absorbed in the fish-keeping hobby.

Selective breeding is undertaken in three major phases which when completed comprise the first cycle of the breeding program. When this stage has been reached, new stock should be introduced and bred to the offspring of the third generation. The three phases of cycle two must now be completed as they were in cycle one.

PHASE ONE

In this phase the initial stock is selected. The fish should be young and the females should be virgins. (If sexually mature males and females are stocked in the same aquarium, the females are not virgins). If such stock is not available from local tropical fish retailers, then seek out other hobbyists who are breeding livebearers. In selecting breeding stock, look for good color patterns, smooth, well-formed body lines and good finnage. It's also important that you don't select your males and females from the same source, for this is likely to produce a brother-sister mating. A brother-sister mating can have disastrous results at a later stage in the program. Make sure the stock is young. Using old fish for breeding stock will thwart the program right from the beginning.

Once the breeding stock is selected, make sure that the males and females are placed in separate tanks. The water in the aquarium in which the females are placed should be newly seasoned and *should be water in which no males have ever resided*. Records have proven that sperm can live for a long time free in the water and that young females can be impregnated at a very early age, even if they may yet be a few weeks away from sexual maturity. Males and females should remain separated, whether their age is known or estimated, until they are a minimum of six months old. During this isolation period they should receive daily a highly nutritious diet comprised of dry foods and small amounts of live or frozen foods, augmented with a daily feeding of live or frozen brine shrimp; live newly-hatched shrimp can be used even for adults.

When the fish are approximately six months old, select the best male and female and place them together in a separate aquarium. If the fish are in good condition the copulatory act will be completed within a few hours, but the pair should be left together until the female's gravid spot darkens in color—this indicates that she is indeed pregnant. The darkening should occur within a week or so. Only one pair should be bred so that the fry from this mating do not become mixed with the fry of another mating. If more than one pair is to be bred then extra aquariums should be set up to avoid mixing the fry. It is really best, though, for the beginning breeder to stick with just one pair. For purposes of identification, the breeders should be considered as the parental generation.

The first batch of young constitutes the first generation in the controlled breeding program. The young should be sexed and the sexes separated at as early an age as possible. Some hobbyists feel that this is necessary to do when the fry are as young as five days of age, but many hobbyists have been quite successful by waiting a few weeks until the fish begin to show more easily visible signs of sex differentiation.

Sexing the fry at five days is not as difficult as it may seem on first thought. Set up a small aquarium of two or two-and-one-half gallons and cover the back of the tank with a piece of black construction paper that has a three-quarter-inch hole cut in its center. Place a goose-neck lamp containing a fairly bright bulb behind the tank so that the light shines through the hole. Place several fry in the tank and with the aid of a magnifying lens look at them closely as they pass in front of the cone of light emanating from the hole in the paper. If they are females, the gravid spot will be seen. Two separate tanks should be set up and ready so that the sexed fish can be separated. Once again, make sure that the tank the females are put into does not contain water that was ever inhabited by any male. Although this method is not 100% accurate, it is accurate enough if the separated young are watched constantly for more overt signs of sex identification as they mature.

As an alternative to sexing young livebearers of five days of age, wait until they are two to three weeks old. At that time the anal fin of the males of most livebearer species will begin to show the first sign of conversion to a gonopodium, as the forward fin rays appear to become thickened. Those that don't show this thickening presumably are females and should be separated out to a tank containing new water. Sometimes, as with almost any animal, there are latent developers, so continue to watch the supposed females for signs of a thickening anal fin. As soon as such fish are spotted they should be moved to the tank containing the males.

It is most important at the beginning of your work with these fishes that accurate records are kept. The number of fry and the age at which they begin to differentiate sexually should be noted. It might also be worthwhile to keep track of the ratio of male to female offspring, since it has been established that water conditions can influence the ratio.

Continuous visual observation is important, not only for detecting latently developing males, but also for detecting fishes with deformities. These should be culled and destroyed as soon as they are noticed. Fishes lacking good color and good growth should also be culled. By continued observation and culling of inferior specimens it is highly probable that only a few of the first generation offspring will remain by the time they have reached the age of six months.

Frequent small feedings of highly nutritious foods are essential during the time when the offspring are maturing. They should be fed as their parents were, using fresh, good quality dry foods, frozen brine shrimp and assorted live foods whenever possible. Newly hatched brine shrimp should be fed to the fry at least once every day. The best way to develop robust young fish is to feed them only a small amount at a time, but feed them five or six times a day. The healthy-looking fishes seen in the wild do not feed once or twice a day but forage for food continuously, all day long. Frequent small feedings in the aquarium simulate this natural condition and seem to produce better fish. Fishes fed in this manner will usually be more colorful and larger than their parents, and this is what the breeder is striving for.

PHASE TWO

During the six-month period when the first generation young are maturing, the original pair (the parental generation) should be maintained separately, each in its own aquarium. It is important that the parental fish be maintained in as good a condition as the fry are maintained, because they will be used again. The female parent fish must be especially well cared for so that she continues to produce young from the first fertilization. Generally, after three to four broods, the female will have used all of the sperm that she has stored from the first fertilization. It is not necessary to save the young of subsequent broods from the first fertilization. In fact, doing so may only add a lot of confusion to your program. Therefore, all fry produced by the parental female subsequent to the first brood and from the first fertilization should be disposed of.

Once the first brood of first generation fry are six months old, the next step in the breeding program can be started. From among the males select the best individual, paying close attention to color pattern, body shape and finnage. Place him in the tank with the parental female. From among the female offspring select the best specimen and place her with the parental father. These two separate matings will produce the second generation. Follow exactly the same plan as that followed for the first generation as far as isolation of the sexes, culling and feeding are concerned. The only change will be that instead of maintaining two aquaria for the fry, you will now maintain four aquaria: one for male offspring of the father-daughter mating, one for female offspring of the father-daughter mating, one for the male offspring of the mother-son mating and one for the female offspring of the mother-son mating.

It is vitally important and imperative that at no time are the fry of the two second generation broods to become mixed with one another; they *must* be maintained as separate broods and eventually as separate sexes of each brood.

PHASE THREE

This is the final stage of the first cycle. When the two batches of second generation offspring have matured, selection is made and the following pairs are placed together for mating.

First pair: A male selected from the father-daughter combination is bred to a female selected from the mother-son combination.

Second pair: A male selected from the mother-son combination is bred to a female selected from the father-daughter combination.

The batches of young from these two matings will constitute the third generation offspring and should be dealt with by the same procedures followed for the second and first generation offspring. It is most important to remember that the first batch of each mating are the only fish to be kept and reared for use in the breeding program.

Controlled breeding using this sort of program has proven beyond a doubt that any of the common aquarium livebearer species can be vastly improved in size, color and body conformity. Dealers at the retail level often buy improved stock from local hobbyists, and as the improvement increases, so does the wholesale price. The breeding of fishes should be undertaken with the same goals in mind as those of bird, dog and cat fanciers . . . improving the quality of the stock. To achieve that improvement it is necessary to follow procedures and systems that have proven successful, especially when trying to improve livebearers. Many well-known breeders of fancy guppies have spent numerous tedious hours developing their superior stock. This required of them a great deal of patience and willingness to accept occasional disappointments. Similarly, breeding any of the exceedingly colorful livebearers, once undertaken by the implementation of these standard practices and principles, assures continuous rewarding results in commensuration for the time and effort expended on such work.

Another appealing aspect of this type of breeding program is that the aquarist controls the amount of additional

1

2

(1) *Xenoophorus captivus* is one of the less colorful goodeids. Photo by H.J. Richter. (2) The long sword on the male swordtail in the center of this photo suggests that it reached sexual maturity at a young age. It will not grow much larger. (3) This guppy has the potential of being developed into an almost solid red strain. (4) The rays anterior to the notch in the anal fin of this red-tailed goodeid, *Xenotoca eiseni*, are the component rays of the gonopodium. Photo by H.J. Richter.

equipment and space required for such an undertaking and therefore can maintain his hobby within an economic level that he can afford.

A final bit of advice on selective breeding relates to the lifespans of livebearers. On the average, most livebearing species live 18 to 24 months. The most desirable period for breeding is between six and 15 months of age. This provides ample time to carry out all of the practices and principles involved in selective breeding. It is common among all fishes but especially the livebearers that the older the female, the greater are the chances that any brood produced will show signs of deterioration. It is therefore an excellent practice to avoid breeding a female that is older than 18 months. Better stock will also be produced by not allowing the females to breed before they are six months old.

HYBRIDIZING

Some of the most beautiful livebearers have been produced by hybridization. For example, the red wagtail strain of the swordtail was the ultimate result of a cross between a platy, *Xiphophorus maculatus,* of the comet variety and a swordtail, *Xiphophorus helleri.* Wagtail platies and swordtails have become true-breeding established strains in the hobby. Many other colorful swordtail and platy strains have also arisen through hybridization.

For the hobbyist who wishes to undertake a hybridization program, it should be realized that the many colorful strains of swordtails and platies that have resulted from hybridizations were not overnight or one generation achievements. Years of careful study and controlled experimentation were undertaken before these colorful fishes became fixed strains. One of the most difficult problems in hybridization is the great percentage of sterility that arises in the hybrid offspring. It takes a great deal of time and patience to overcome this problem, but apparently it can be overcome.

However, for the average aquarist, improvement of the present varieties of any livebearer is far more important than developing new strains through selective hybridization. Hybridization is more of an undertaking for the experienced aquarist who has not only the complex facilities necessary but also the required knowledge of the principles involved.

This is the lyretail black molly. It was probably developed from black *Poecilia sphenops*. Many hobbyists have found this strain not as hardy as some of the plainer-finned black mollies. Photo by R. Zukal.

A young female topsail platy. The platies below may be the result of a cross between *Xiphophorus maculatus* and *X. variatus.* These two species have been so thoroughly interbred that it is often difficult to recognize the form of the parents. Photo below courtesy of Wardley Products, Co.

Selecting Livebearers

The selection of livebearers given in the following pages lists only a few of the many species known and lists many different strains of most of the popular livebearers. In compiling this list primary consideration was given to color patterns, temperament and habits, and availability. The selection discussed provides an ample array of fishes, thus giving the ardent enthusiast a wide choice of strains to improve upon or hybridize with for the production of new strains.

There is an enormous opportunity for all aquarists to specialize in one or more species or even in one color variety of a particular species. The choice of fish and the depth to which one wishes to delve are virtually unlimited, and

all that is required is the patience and tenacity to overcome a few disappointing failures along the way, failures from which a lot can be learned. Once the aquarist undertakes an earnest effort toward a more scientific approach, an immediate increase of interest and enthusiasm results and the rewards are far beyond the expectations of most aquarists.

GUPPIES

The guppy, *Poecilia reticulata,* was originally described by Peters in 1859 from specimens taken in the Rio Guayne in Caracas, Venezuela. He called the fish *Girardinus reticulatus.* Later, A.C.L. Guenther of the British Museum (Natural History) described some fish brought back from Trinidad by the Reverend Robert John Lechmere Guppy. Guenther described the fish as *Girardinus guppii* in honor of Reverend Guppy, while recognizing the fish described earlier by Peters from Venezuela as a full species, *G. reticulata.* It was from Guenther's chosen name for this fish that the common name guppy arose.

Distribution: The fact that the guppy has been described under no less than 13 different scientific names attests to the great natural variability and broad distribution of this fish and provides us with a clue as to its potential for producing new strains. The guppy was originally found in the area north of the Amazon River, in northern Brazil, Venezuela, Guyana, Trinidad and Barbados. Now, however, because of its worldwide popularity and because of its use in mosquito control, it has been released and has become established in tropical and subtropical climates all over the world. Recent reports of guppies being found in natural waters have come from as far away as Australia. In all of these areas of the world guppies are found in slow-flowing streams, ponds and ditches in either freshwater or brackish water habitats.

Coloration and form: To say that guppies have come a long way from their wild progenitors would be a tremendous understatement. Guppies were originally described as having iridescent lateral scales of various colors overlying a basic brownish green background color. A variety of black, yellow, brown and reddish spots of various sizes and shapes was seen on occasional specimens. Of male guppies it was at one time said that no two ever looked alike. Females from any locality, however, looked basically the same, a drab brownish olive-green color with no spots and very little iridescence.

Guppy standards: Guppy breeders have formed local organizations all over the world, and even an International Fancy Guppy Association (IFGA) has been formed. Through the joint efforts of all of these groups, standards for color patterns, fin shapes and body proportions have been established. These standards are rigidly adhered to by sanctioned judges at shows all over the world. The standards are well known, and any guppy breeder worth his salt tries to adhere to these standards in developing and showing his own strains of guppies.

At least 26 show classifications have been developed by the IFGA. Guppies are classed by body color, color pattern on the body, eye color, tail type, combination of body color and tail color and tail color. There are, of course, a variety of acceptable sub-classes within each classification. Some of the 26 classifications apply only to female guppies and are based mainly on color varieties. Judging standards include points for body size, body shape, body color and body condition as well as points for color, shape and condition of the dorsal fin and color, size, shape and condition of the caudal fin. Points are also given for deportment and symmetry.

Maintenance and breeding: Much of the detail on maintenance and breeding of guppies was discussed earlier in this book in the general discussion of livebearers. There are, however, some important details to be noted that apply specifically to guppies. The gestation period of the guppy is four to six weeks, but, as with the other livebearers, the ex-

1

2

(1) These red guppies won first place in a Russian guppy competition. (2) Consistent reproducibility of the color pattern is what most guppy breeders strive for. Photos 1 and 2 by H. Kyselov. (3) These strange eyes belong to a "four-eyed" livebearer *Anableps anableps*. This species can see quite well out of the water and underwater at the same time thanks to the unique structure of its eyes. Photo by W. Twomey. (4) Two well matched ¾ black deltatail guppies. Photo by Midge Hill.

act time depends upon food, temperature, age and size of the female and other general environmental factors. Approximately 20 to 100 fry are born in one brood, but this, too, depends greatly upon the size of the female, her age and other environmental factors.

If well fed, young guppies grow very quickly, showing overt signs of sex as early as three weeks of age. Guppies are sexually mature at two months of age, but they are not usually full grown until they are six months old.

Guppies are quite tolerant of salt in the water which is no doubt related to the fact that in the wild they are often found in brackish water habitats. In fact, guppies can be acclimated and bred in a marine aquarium.

Most guppy breeders keep and breed their stock at temperatures in the mid seventies. They can be kept at warmer temperatures which will help force their growth, but this also shortens their lifespan. Guppies raised in water in the high 70's and low 80's pass their reproductive prime very quickly and show signs of old age before guppies raised in cooler water even reach their prime.

Much more detailed information on breeding, raising and showing guppies can be found in Lou Wasserman's book *How to Raise Show Guppies*.

MOLLIES

Mollies have always been very popular in the tropical fish hobby, especially among beginners. This particularly applies to the magnificent black strains. This great popularity is rather surprising considering the fact that mollies are generally the most delicate of the popular livebearing aquarium species. The problems caused by this delicateness do not occur exclusively among hobbyists or even beginning hobbyists; many wholesalers and retailers also experience difficulties in maintaining mollies.

In the chapter "The Aquarium Environment" it was mentioned that mollies and guppies are often found in a brackish water environment. This is especially so with mollies. As a matter of fact, some aquarists have had great success keeping and breeding mollies in full-strength marine water. Even highly domesticated strains such as those having a rich velvety black pigmentation are very successfully kept in marine water. The use of at least some salt in the water of mollies is very important in preventing the difficulties normally experienced with these fishes.

Although mollies are omnivorous fishes (they consume both animal and vegetable matter), many of the problems experienced with these fishes stem from a lack of adequate vegetable matter in the diet. Mollies require more vegetable matter than any of the other popular livebearer species.

The final factor in achieving success with mollies is the avoidance of sudden temperature drops of more than a degree or two. While most popular livebearers are very sensitive to chill, the problem is most critical with mollies. A sudden temperature drop of two degrees Fahrenheit can start mollies shimmying.

The most popular mollies are black mollies. So many different strains of black mollies have been developed that it would not be possible to describe the history of them all in a book of this type. Yucatans, perma-blacks and black sailfins have been the most popularized black molly types. None of the black mollies are found as all-black fish in nature, except for occasional sports. It is from such black sports and subsequent careful line-breeding that most all-black mollies were derived. In addition, many black mollies were derived from carefully planned crosses between different molly species. After many generations of crosses and line-breeding programs true-breeding black molly strains came about.

One of the most well known molly species is *Poecilia sphenops*. There is little doubt that most of the black mollies available to hobbyists today are derived at least in part from this species. It is known that black sailfin mollies have been

2

(1) A most unique and highly sought after live-bearer is the black sailfin molly. Photo by H.J. Richter. (2) Black mollies are quite prolific when raised in outdoor pools. (3) Sailfin mollies having a high amount of red pigment are being developed in the Orient. Photo by Y.W. Ong.

3

produced by crossing *P. sphenops* with sailfin species such as *P. latipinna* or more rarely *P. velifera*. These crosses have produced some of the most magnificent mollies ever known to the hobby.

Mollies having a black and white marbled pattern are also quite common in the hobby. A marbled *Poecilia sphenops* very often has a bright orange border on the outer edge of its caudal fin. It has been the experience of many hobbyists that the marbled strains are quite a bit hardier than the all-black strains. Marbled sailfin mollies are also occasionally seen. They are probably derived from crosses between *P. sphenops* and *P. latipinna*.

Several fin shapes are now being bred into fishes derived from *P. sphenops, P. latipinna* and *P. velifera*. Black lyretail mollies are seen quite frequently in pet shops. While they are very handsome fishes with their unusual lyre-shaped tail, they generally seem to lack the deep rich black color so often seen in other *P. sphenops* derivatives. Lyretail black mollies often have elongated dorsal, anal and pelvic fins, too.

Several attempts have been made to develop a deltatail black molly. These have not met with much success as far as producing them in commercial quantities is concerned.

Poecilia velifera is the other fairly popular sailfin molly species. It occurs mainly in the coastal areas of Yucatan and grows to a length of six to seven inches, quite a bit bigger than *P. latipinna*. The spots in the dorsal sail of this fish are not interconnected as they are in *P. latipinna*, and they are rounder. Of all the mollies available to the aquarist, hobbyists find this species to be the most sensitive to environmental upset. Therefore, in keeping *P. velifera*, the conditions prescribed for the maintenance of mollies must be more rigidly adhered to than for any other molly species.

No matter which strain of molly you choose to keep, remember to provide the fishes with plenty of greens in the diet, keep their water conditions very stable and add at least one tablespoon of salt to each gallon of aquarium water. Adhering to these conditions will usually eliminate most of the problems normally encountered in keeping and breeding mollies.

Because there has been so much crossbreeding in the production of today's molly strains, it would be difficult to produce an accurate figure for the gestation period and the brood size of most domesticated mollies. In general, the gestation period for these fishes ranges from about six weeks to about three months, and as many as 200 young can be produced in one brood. As with other livebearer species, a lot of this depends upon the age and size of the female as well as environmental conditions such as diet, temperature, etc.

SWORDTAILS

The green swordtail, *Xiphophorus helleri,* is the naturally occurring swordtail species from which, by careful line-breeding and hybridizing with other *Xiphophorus* species, most of the highly colorful domesticated swordtail varieties were developed. Much of the color has been introduced into this species by crossing it with various color varieties of the platy which, by and large, has more naturally occurring color patterns than the swordtail.

In addition to color patterns, there have been two distinct forms of finnage developed in swordtails. One of them, the Simpson swordtail, was developed by Mrs. Thelma Simpson of California. She found some mutants among her swordtail stock that had high dorsal fins. As the result of careful selective breeding of these mutants, a true-breeding "hifin" strain was developed which ultimately became known as the Simpson swordtail. By hybridization and further selective breeding this hifin trait has been introduced into other *Xiphophorus* species such as the platy, *X. maculatus,* and the variatus, *X. variatus.*

The other fin form commonly seen in swordtails is the

1

2

(1) Although the wagtail pattern has been bred into green swordtails, they are not commonly seen. Photo by K. Quitshau. (2) Red wagtail swordtails are very common in pet shops. Photo by Dr. Herbert R. Axelrod. (3) This all red molly was developed in Singapore by Tan Guk Eng. (4) The lyretail golden sailfin molly was also developed by Tan Guk Eng. Photos 3 and 4 by Y.W. Ong.

lyretail. In this form both the upper and the lower rays of the caudal fin are elongated. The form first showed up as a mutant in the aquaria of a Florida fish farmer, Don Adams. He also, through careful selective breeding, was able to produce a true-breeding strain. However, in most cases the strain can only be bred true by artificial insemination, because the mutation produces, in addition to elongated rays in the caudal fin, elongated anterior rays in the dorsal fin, the pelvic fins and the anal fin. The latter produces an enormously long gonopodium which renders the males incapable of fertilizing a female except when a female by chance takes in some sperm that are free in the water. Artificial insemination has proven that these males are fertile; they are just incapable of delivering their sperm packets to a female by normal means.

Most of the color forms in swordtails have at one time or another been combined with the hifin trait and the lyretail trait. These combinations have produced some spectacularly beautiful swordtails. For example, one can find cherry red, yellow or green tuxedo lyretail swordtails. Red and yellow hifin tuxedo and non-tuxedo swordtails are also available. There is a hifin strain combining red and yellow in the same fish; it is sometimes known as the pineapple or pineapple hifin swordtail. Like most of the popular livebearers, true-breeding albinos have been developed in swordtails, too.

Swordtails that have not departed from their wild progenitors very much in color and form, for instance green swordtails, are not very difficult to keep. They don't require water quite as warm as that recommended for mollies. Swordtails are quite comfortable at 72 to 75°F, probably because in nature they are found mostly in the cooler waters of lakes, lagoons and slow-flowing rivers in Mexico, whereas mollies are usually found in warmer coastal waters. Swordtails do quite well without the addition of salt to the water, although a teaspoonful per gallon of water seems to add a bit to their general good health and deportment. They are not as susceptible to disease resulting from temperature shock as some other livebearers.

Some of the fancier strains of swordtails are not as hardy as the greens or hardier reds. They must be handled almost as carefully as one would handle a delicate lyretail molly in terms of cleanliness and stability of the aquarium environment. Moderately hard water having a pH of 6.8 to about 7.4 suits most swordtails quite well. As with most aquarium fishes, partial water changes should be made weekly.

In purchasing swordtails, males having delayed "sword" development usually turn out to be larger, sturdier specimens than those having full "sword" development at a smaller size. This is because the growth rate slows down considerably once all of the sexual characteristics are fully developed. More often than among any of the other "big four" livebearers, male swordtails tend to get into some serious fights with one another. Therefore, it is imperative if a trio is being kept that it consist of only one male and two females. If swordtails are kept in a larger group, it is also important that females outnumber males by approximately a two to one ratio.

A gestation period of four to six weeks is common in most *Xiphophorus* species. Brood size can range up to 200 young, although there are records of female swordtails producing over 240 young in a single brood.

PLATIES

Platies are found primarily in lowland waters on the Atlantic slopes of Central America in places where the water temperatures remain fairly cool for most of the year. Like swordtails, platies do well in the aquarium in water kept in the mid to low 70's. They also like the water moderately hard with a pH of 6.8 to 7.4. In other words, ordinary tapwater suits these fishes just fine.

Platies have an extremely variable black pattern on a

1

2

(1) This closeup of the mouth of *Belonesox belizanus* clearly shows why it is not a good fish for a community aquarium. Photo by H.J. Richter. (2) A lateral view of *Anableps anableps* shows how it positions itself for simultaneous vision above and below the water surface. Photo by Dr. Herbert R. Axelrod at the Berlin Aquarium. (3) Golden sailfin mollies are one of the more delicate molly strains. (4) The hifin variatus platy, *Xiphophorus variatus*. Photo by S. Kochetov.

yellowish brown to bluish gray body. Occasionally patches of red appear on wild fish. It is from fish such as these that many of today's brilliantly colored platies were developed. Over the years it has become apparent that there are few limits to the variety that can be developed in platy color patterns. All of the true-breeding color patterns seen in domesticated platies are basically the same as those appearing in domesticated swordtails. This is because, as mentioned earlier, hybridizations between some of these colorful platies and plainer green swordtails resulted ultimately in colorful swordtails. Conversely, the long dorsal fin conformation and the extended anterior fin ray conformation in platies seem to have been derived from hybridizations with swordtails having these fin conformations.

Like swordtails, highly inbred and fancy strains of platies are quite susceptible to disease when exposed to environmental pollution or fluctuation that is not mild. On the other hand, strains such as the blue platy or the yellow crescent platy seem to be quite hardy in the aquarium.

VARIATUS

Although scientists often include *Xiphophorus variatus* in the *maculatus* grouping, the body of these colorful fish resembles more that of a swordtail than a platy. The fish is widely distributed in the cooler lowland waters of Mexico, and of all the *Xiphophorus* species, its optimum temperature is the lowest, being around 70°F.

Though the variatus resembles the swordtail in body form, the males do not grow a "sword." In addition, it is a smaller fish than the swordtail. Males, for instance, reach a length of about two inches, whereas male swordtails reach a length of about three inches. Female variatus grow to about three inches, but female swordtails can reach a length of four-and-a-half inches.

When comparing swordtails and variatus for color in their natural forms, one finds that variatus are much more colorful. In nature, variatus show a yellowish orange to yellowish green color on the front part of the body and an olive-greenish to bluish color toward the rear. At the center of the body there are four to twelve (depending upon which subspecies one is dealing with) dark vertical bars. The caudal fin is yellow and sometimes has a reddish tint. Some even have a black border along the posterior edge of this fin. Females are generally colored about the same in pattern but are not nearly as brilliant as the males.

Other color varieties have been introduced into this fish as has the long dorsal fin trait which in platies and variatus is often called the "topsail" trait rather than the hifin trait as it is called in swordtails. This fish has often been hybridized with platies and swordtails and may have had a large part in the production of bright colors in both of those *Xiphophorus* species.

Of all the *Xiphophorus* species, *X. variatus* in its natural form or in domesticated forms not too far removed from its wild progenitors is by far the hardiest. As a matter of fact this fish may well be the hardiest of all common aquarium livebearers.

OTHER LIVEBEARERS

There are a few other livebearers that deserve brief mention in this book, because they do occasionally show up in shops or in the tanks of hobbyists. One that has become well known in the late 1970's is the goodeid (belonging to the family Goodeidae mentioned in the chapter on reproduction) *Xenotoca eiseni*. This interesting livebearer is shaped something like a platy through the middle and anterior part of its body, but the caudal peduncle is extremely narrow from top to bottom compared to that of the platy. The fish is a dull brownish yellow color with a bluish black band running from the eye through the caudal peduncle in the female and partially through the caudal peduncle in the male. The posterior part of the male's caudal peduncle is reddish orange to cherry red.

1

2

3

(1) Except for the golden color, these comet platies closely resemble wild comet platies. Photo by M.F. Roberts. (2) This male platy shows the Mickey Mouse pattern on the caudal peduncle. Photo by S. Frank. (3) *Heterandria formosa*, the smallest livebearer native to the U.S. Photo by R. Zukal. 4. A *Gambusia* species. Photo by R. Zukal. 5. A courting pair of red platies. Photo by R. Zukal.

The red-tailed goodeid, as *X. eiseni* is commonly known, requires moderately hard water but can tolerate a wide variety of pH values. It requires water temperatures in the low to mid 80's. Its dietary requirements are about the same as those of the poeciliids discussed in this book.

What is most interesting about this fairly hardy fish is its method of reproduction which, contrary to that of poeciliids, is quite similar to that of mammals in terms of embryonic nutrition. The young develop within the female in a uterine-like structure. For at least the latter part of their embryonic development they obtain nutrition from the mother through a cord attached to each embryo. The young are born with the cord and some placenta-like material attached to the abdomen. This is dropped off within 24 hours and the ½-inch young are then able to swim and feed freely.

Another livebearer occasionally seen in the hobby is the halfbeak. There are several genera and species of halfbeaks known to the hobby, but the most well-known is *Dermogenys pusillus*. It is found in fresh and brackish waters in streams, ponds and pools of many parts of Southeast Asia. It has a pike-like appearance, but the lower jaw protrudes out well beyond the upper jaw, hence the name halfbeak.

Halfbeaks, although predatory as far as their feeding habits are concerned, are shy fishes that prefer to hide among clumps of floating or overhanging vegetation. In nature they feed on insects that fall or light on the water, and these fishes are not capable of feeding from the bottom. An ideal food for captive halfbeaks is vestigial-winged fruitflies which are easily cultured in small bottles (see *Encyclopedia of Live Foods* by Charles O. Masters).

One of the most predatory livebearers known to the hobby is the pike livebearer or pike top minnow, *Belonesox belizanus*. Like the "big four" livebearers, this fish belongs to the family Poeciliidae. It is found in the backwaters of rivers, in lakes and in marshes along the Atlantic slope of

Central America. Males reach a length of five to six inches and females grow as long as eight to nine inches, making this species the largest of all the poeciliids. Not only do these fish prey on other species, but they also prey upon each other, especially the females. It is not uncommon for a female to swallow her own mate.

No book on livebearers could be complete without some mention of the oddball *Anableps anableps,* commonly known as four-eyes. This name comes from the odd shape of the eyes. The cornea is divided by a horizontal dark band and the pupil has a figure-eight shape. Thus when cruising at the surface with the eyes protruding slightly from the water, the fish can see above and below the surface of the water at the same time. The advantages to a surface-dwelling fish of this kind of vision are obvious.

In the wild, four-eyes reaches almost 12 inches but rarely reaches that length in captivity. It does well in water kept in the high 70's to low 80's, and it should be kept in a shallow tank that is tightly covered so as to enclose a warm humid atmosphere over the water. It thrives well in brackish water but will do well in 100% seawater, too. Meaty foods such as frozen shrimp will be taken if they float for a while. Live terrestrial insects such as grasshoppers or cockroaches dropped into the aquarium will be devoured without delay. The fish reaches sexual maturity at a length of about six inches and the young are born at a length of nearly 1¼ inches. They eat newly hatched brine shrimp that are attracted to the surface by an overhead lamp.

There are many other livebearers that can be kept in an aquarium successfully, but because of the size limitations of this book they cannot all be covered here. For a very detailed account of the taxonomy, ecology, habits, breeding techniques and color strains of the livebearers covered here and many many more, it is recommended that the reader see *Livebearing Aquarium Fishes* by Kurt Jacobs.